A Strange Heart

Winner of the 1995 Marianne Moore Poetry Prize

The Marianne Moore Poetry Prize was established in 1991 by Helicon Nine Editions, and is awarded annually to an unpublished manuscript chosen by a distinguished poet through a nationwide competition.

The judge for 1995 was James Tate.

A Strange Heart

Poems
Jane O. Wayne

Missouri Center
for the Book

Missouri Authors
Collection

HELICON NINE EDITIONS
KANSAS CITY, MISSOURI

All rights reserved under International and Pan American Copyright
Conventions. Published by Helicon Nine Editions, a division of
Midwest Center for the Literary Arts, Inc.,
P. O. Box 22412, Kansas City, MO 64113.
Requests to copy any part of this work should be addressed to the publisher.

Grateful acknowledgment is made to the editors of the following magazines
in which these poems first appeared:
The American Scholar, Confrontation, Crosscurrents, The Iowa Review,
The Journal of the American Medical Association, The Michigan Quarterly, Poetry,
Poetry Northwest, Reconstructionist, Sagarin Review, Southern Poetry Review,
Tar River Poetry, The Webster Review, Yankee, Poetry Miscellany; and in
the anthologies, *A Light in the Mind* and *Anthology of Missouri Women Writers.*

Cover painting: Sam Wayne, *Red Chair at a Window.*
Book design: Tim Barnhart.

Partial funding for this book was provided by
the National Endowment for the Arts, a federal agency,
the Missouri Arts Council and the Kansas Arts Commission, state agencies;
and the N.W. Dible Foundation.

Library of Congress Cataloging-in-Publication Data

Wayne. Jane O.
  A strange heart : poems / Jane O. Wayne. -- 1st ed.
      p.   cm.
  ISBN 1-884235-18-2 (alk. paper)
  I. Title.
PS3573.A94S77 1996
811' .54- -dc20   96-8435
                                                                          CIP

Second Printing, 1998
Printed in the United States of America.
HELICON NINE EDITIONS • P. O. Box 22412 • Kansas City, MO 64113

For Ursula and Justine

Contents

A Strange Heart

Kiyomizu

The sun beats down. The gravel path curves
like an empty river-bed where all afternoon
we drift among the parasols.

What I can't remember
about the temple grounds and the heat
I imagine—until after twenty years

I can't tell one from the other,
his oars pulling the water, her fan pulling air.
And those pines on the hill, those dark paintings

on sky blue—do we really notice them
or do we read it afterwards: each tree shaped,
each bud between a thumb and finger?

The path curves. The sun beats down
on the gravel. The wooden floors still creak
inside the temple. They're smooth and cool

against our feet. But did we leave our shoes
on the steps, or do we imagine it?
Pines, parasols, pagodas.

The path curves. The sun beats down. We stand
in line for water, taking turns:
only one fountain, one bamboo cup.

In September

At the kitchen table
you trim the string beans,
green fingers snapping in the air
between your fingers. They call us
to attention as if we were children
dozing through a lesson.

How easily we're caught off guard:
the door letting the dog out,
letting the cold night in;
and those brown leaves spreading in the elm
like moth holes in a sweater.
The old betrayals never lose their chill.

We should know by now.
We heard the slow music of the green,
of waving motions—the sprinkler sweeping
through the air, its watery arch
like the children on the swing
or the newspaper fanning near your face.

Yet we carved the ripeness on each plate
so carelessly, spit out the minutes
with the watermelon seeds.
We didn't count the vases full
of long-stemmed days, those afternoons
that we let sink slowly

into canvas chairs, the weightlessness
of heat, working on us,
working on the plum tree.
One by one, we let all our cares
fall from us, let the fruit sprawl,
soft and purple on the ground.

So what if the nights are longer now

or if the folded lawn chairs
lean against the stone wall in our basement.
Should we have held on,
tap-rooted like a dandelion,
to each earthy moment?

Isoptera

Suddenly they were streaming
down the porch steps, thousands
of them, white wings, dark bodies,
the size of tiny moths.
They kept bubbling out of that space
between the steps, for ten minutes
pouring steadily, like water
from a tap that won't turn off.

Ignoring us,
our waving hands, our voices,
even our feet next to them,
they kept sliding down the stairs,
against the dark wood floor
the pale swarm like some lace scarf
slipping out of a drawer,
out of our reach.

When it reached the last step
what else could we do
but watch the cloth rippling,
lifting from the ground
in a wind we couldn't feel,
then over the lawn, over the flower beds,
the fabric all at once disintegrating,
white shreds filling the air, like ashes.

Drinking Tea at Dusk

So what if they coax us
to the table, distracting us
with cards and tea.
We know what they're after
with their clicking heels
and snapping fingers,
their dark-eyed song,
the dance that spirals closer.
We know all their ruses:
the sleight of hand,
the cunning smile
that can turn a heart
or pocket inside out.
There's no stopping them,
no outstaring them.
They want to take our empty cups
and read the future
in the dregs.

Inheritance

We thought we could change our ways,
could turn an old coat
inside-out and get a new one.

We thought we could learn
from their mistakes, discern a pattern,
break a code. But we were wrong.

This is the secret we kept from ourselves,
the wrong letter in our envelope
with no return address.

There's no avoiding it. We spread
a threadbare linen on the dinner table;
the truth shows through.

Our genes are worse than habits.
They're the rank vines
tangled in the privet hedge,

the barking down the street
that we can't silence from a bed.
They're the hand-me-downs:

the dent in the pot,
the cracked plate that shudders
when we set it down.

Years ago behind closed doors
they made up their minds about us,
cast their votes in every cell.

Door-smilers, handshakers,
they're the uninvited guests
who get past our objections.

Their feet up on our best furniture,
their ashes on the floor—
we can't get rid of them.

Going in for Tests

In a glass cubicle
someone takes your name
and your address, then
at the bottom of the page
you sign your life away.
Someone else behind a desk
has your number, bands your wrist
like a pigeon's leg—
but you're not flying off.
Your shoes, your street clothes gone,
you match the walls
in your pale uniform. You surrender
to the bed, the lone inmate
in this boxcar of a room.
Door closed, train in motion—
on this trip there's no turning back,
no way around the sentry at the gate
who signals those ahead of you,
thumb up or down,
as if he's just directing traffic.
All night you're getting closer—
on your left side
the guard dog snarls.

Waiting Room

Day-old, the tulips mope in a vase.
Like wounds, they've already turned
a dryer, darker red.
And these skin-pink chairs
meant to comfort, don't.
Their plush upholstery nettles the flesh,
rankles the foot-tapping out of us.
Instead of windows,
two glassed-in photographs suffice—
and overhead three fluorescent tubes drone,
like dotards, to themselves.
Beige walls, beige carpeting,
rubber plants stifling the air—
who could bear it?
By morning, I'm all bones
at odds with sockets in my chair.
Even the sympathies start to screech
their chalk across a blackboard.
They keep trying to soothe,
trying to put the grape back on its stem.

Intensive Care

Even the smallest tide
in the silver sea of a thermometer
can turn a ship around.

On that bleak shore,
every ebb and flow was charted.
What else was there to go on? Breathing

and nothing else but breathing—
no more than what an ear can conjure
out of an empty conch.

In such a storm, we might have been villagers
waiting for a lost ship.
We could never rest.

Which is worse then—waves beating
on an empty beach or the throbs of that device
working for your heart?

For months, it went on: no let up,
no north star in that blank sky—
only nods, grimaces,

your open eyes taunting us, like some word
on the tip of the tongue
one agonizes to recall but can't.

Day after day, on the same narrow coast,
we stood guard, waiting
for some speck to reappear, for the wind

to give a different verdict.
To get through the nights,
we let the flat horizon hypnotize us.

On the Heart List

He's sound asleep,
mesmerized by pumping,
so he doesn't know
what "heartless" means—
how, like a crow,
it hovers single-mindedly, waiting
for someone else's loss,
how, always on alert, its wife sleeps
near the telephone,
twists and tangles in her sheets
and, all night, dreams
of crashes, dreams by accident
the heart that saves him
is his daughter's.
He doesn't know how much she fears
the nightmare, like some Judith
rising up in her, sword in hand,
how even in the daylight
she fears the dark, the wrong head
severed on the sand.

Waking Up

What else fell when the shears snapped
around the flower stem?
In the sheets, the smell of loss lingers

medicinal and sharp,
as the antiseptic on a cut.
This must be what an addict feels

under his tongue, his fingernails—
no detour, nothing to chew on.
Everything is different now.

With the curtains closed, I can't tell
the morning from the night, the ocean
from an empty shell.

A whole spring and summer in this cubicle—
like a winter coat in a closet!
To my own flesh, then, I'm a revenant—

or is this someone else's dream
that I've stumbled into, the way a drunk
enters the wrong house in the dark?

If I could, I'd roll over
into the cooler place in bed.
Or should I pretend it's home—the room

inside the mirror on the wall
where everything is backward, where
I'm a distant rumor of myself?

Tubes, like parasitic vines, dangle
from my mouth and limbs.
They're trying to win me over.

Anaesthesia

How dark the water was,
when I dipped the oars
their pale hands disappeared.
I must have lost a year of nights
drifting on that lake.
While I slept, I might have been the cortex
in a tree, the bark around me
toughening, the wooden circles
widening their grasp.
I might have been enchanted in my bed,
might have let them steal my heart
and leave another.
What really happened?
Did I fall asleep under an elder tree
or is this the madness
of a strange heart pounding in my chest?
And in what forest of imagination
am I sleeping now?

The Retrieval

To picture that day,
you have to stand above your own sleep
until you are only a shadow
that falls across a table,
the nearly-drowned they're getting ready
to pull out of the deep.
Sometimes you go back
to that shock of pinkish-gray
in a jar on the vet's shelf
or for the shape
you conjure up a hybrid form
that someone holds mid-air,
a cross between a valentine
and some hot-water bottle
that's not quite full, that you imagine
lukewarm to the touch and flopping slightly
in those upturned palms.
Then suddenly—
as if you opened your eyes
when the gloved hands lifted it out of you
and someone else poured ice water
into the red basin of your chest—
there's a moment
when, like sugar sprinkled onto frothy milk,
it sits lightly on your mind
before it sinks.

Filling the Terrarium

Coming back
when we crossed the creek
I didn't know that the hours
we had spent walking in those woods
were already as slippery
as the mud-banks under our feet.

I didn't remember
till we got inside, till after
I put dirt in this large jar
and picked up the moss again—
how furry it was and limp
like a sleeping animal

how when I first lifted it
it let go so readily
no more hold on that log
than we had on our afternoon
or on the moss itself
as we water it and tighten the lid.

Walking into the Wind

On a cold, drab day like this,
wherever we walk, the dogs follow us
along an empty street
in a part of town that wasn't on the map.
They hound us in our coats and hats,
that rib-thin pack,
nosing for garbage in the gutter,
eyeing us on a shadowless day.

And those urchins, three or four of them,
outside that pension—is it the wind
that brings them back,
cheering, scampering on the pavement,
their bare feet leathery and cracked?
They keep kicking a torn soccer ball between them,
crossing the street, crossing my mind.
That cold thud still bounces in the wind.

From one winter to the next
we climb a winding street,
breathing fumes of kerosene
from a fire we can't see.
Our collars up,
our fingers thick in gloves again,
we're wrapped in the wool of the past,
a layer of snow, a layer of remembering.

Sometimes before we cross a creek
I can hear the ice buckling
over the stones again
and that white dog rattling in the leaves.
If we come to a pond in the woods,
he'll lift his head, and the wolf in him
will howl at a child skating alone,
circling a pond frozen in memory.

Undertones

In bed—the windows open
all those summer nights ago—
sometimes, if she lay still enough,
she could hear the richest part
of someone else's conversation
floating over the lawns, a wordless hum
the branches sifted—pure
and unencumbered in the air.

Upstairs, she learned to listen
for their muffled talk, its lure
like messages in unsealed envelopes.
Even half-asleep, she held on
to that loose murmuring
around her in the dark—its soft shield
like the sheet she pulls over herself
on the hottest nights.

Summer Skirmishes

There was a war on,
if you listened to the radio,
but our neighborhood was quiet that summer.
In the morning when the milk-wagon stopped
you could hear bottles clinking
in the metal carrier, the horse's tail
swishing flies away. We used to follow
the wagon from house to house,
watching its marvel in the heat—
those cakes of ice,
always wet, always solid.

Sometimes when the milkman
stopped outside our house,
he would chip off ice for us to chew,
his pick attacking like a bayonet
out of our comic-books. How unexpectedly
the ice, then, would torture us,
its smooth surface turn to needles
in our hands, and when we dropped the ice
near the curb, how easily
we dropped our pain
on that tree-lined street.

Made in India

To take up the hem in this dress
first I have to rip out
someone else's handwork, stitch
by stitch, cutting and pulling
what someone else has sewn
in double thread, in catch-stitches.
Was it that barefoot tailor
cross-legged on the floor
who stood to greet us
in a back room on a back street
in Baroda? Or was it in Ahmedebad
in the bazaar—the skull-capped vendor
who beckoned toothlessly
from a stall full of cloth, behind him
that machine he cranked by hand,
those bright stacks lined up
like crayons in a box?
The thread keeps snapping at me.
Who else held this purple cotton in my lap,
pulled this hemline taut
between a thumb and finger as I do?
Was it those two men we photographed—
thin legs, thin smiles,
hunkering in dhotis,
their purple hands stretching out
a sheet like this to dry
on the pavement in Udaipur?
I circle slowly,
pulling threads that are knotted
at both ends, opening a hem
like an old envelope.

The Knot

On Monday after she strips the bed
she can hear the sheets
sliding down the clothes chute,
can feel the suction of another week
whooshing from her hands.
She knows how another morning
can slip over her head, how mindlessly
she can button up the front
and thinly powdering the facts,
can let the frown pass in the mirror.

No appetite, no zest:
she's full of sameness, had enough
of the bland diet of routine—its place
set at her table, its black coffee
in her cup. She keeps rubbing the ring
out of the bath tub, peeling
the same potato, changing the sheets.
She can't change her life:
the harder she pulls,
the tighter the knot of habit.

Invisible Devils

"The air is not so full of flies in summer as it is at all times
of invisible devils, this Paracelsus stiffly maintains. . . ."
—Robert Burton, *The Anatomy of Melancholy*

You can be walking down a street
in rush hour and out of nowhere
that awful fluttering arrives—that shadow

with its perfect aim singling you out
on the sidewalk. Without warning,
those wide wings can swoop down,

those talons haul you by the scruff
out of the narrow canyon of your ways.
Even in a crowded grocery store,

some demon that you never see
can attack again and leave you
weaving slowly up and down an aisle

like someone without a list,
lost behind a heavy shopping cart
in a maze of labels.

Half-way home when your car stops
along the highway and the door
swings open on the frozen field,

you can fall out of yourself
with a snap—your grip
no better than a defective seat belt.

You once thought you were as safe
as the good china locked in your cabinet,
but nothing can save you.

Wherever you hide, the wolf
sniffs you out. He huffs and puffs
at all your walls, like so much straw.

Headache

In this room, the old wallpaper
bleeds through the paint,
blackbirds caught in flight.

Whoever looks through these windows
knows you can't escape,
knows the knock at the door

that won't take "no" for an answer.
You can hear a tongue rasping
in an empty bowl,

the slow circles of a tiger.
You pour another glass of wine,
but it won't go away.

It takes your reading chair,
your bed. It occupies your pillow.
In the dark, you try ignoring it

but it gets rough with you.
This is the same growl
that followed you home last week,

the same lead pipe
in the mugger's hand
that won't hear reason.

In a Fix

She's vehement, shakes her head
the way you would a hat to get
the snow or rain off. But nothing happens.

She can't get away from it,
can't crumple it and toss it in the trash
like some candy wrapper.

The cat keeps coming back, claws out,
working and reworking the same spot.
It won't scare off.

Downstairs, the wind lifts
and drops the transom by the hour,
someone rising and sitting,

praying to no one. Her empty house
is full of obsessions, hard to kill
as flies diving at the table.

She tries one chair, then another,
but they're all wrong, whispering
their incessant nonsense in her ears,

like air-bubbles in the aquarium.
All day, the fish keep surfacing—
top-feeders that nothing can satisfy.

She spins the dial,
changing stations on the radio,
but nothing can change her mind.

If the door-knocker does go away,
he'll just come back tomorrow:
a different shirt, the same insistence.

She can't close the window
on the screeching katydid, can't stop
the dervish of a thought from whirling.

Prone to Worry

Out of a sound sleep
a thought he didn't know he had
turns against him,
seizes him, head to toe,
like a muscle cramp.

Twisting sheets, throwing blankets
to the floor, he's at it again:
the back and forth of worry
like windshield wipers
on a spot that won't rub off.

No map, no moon—he's run off course,
broken down in a tough neighborhood
of the mind, a back street
where anything can happen after dark,
any thought can hit and run.

He gets nowhere on his mattress
rolling helplessly
like a pencil in someone else's hand.
No matter what he does,
he can't get comfortable, can't sleep.

One by one, his spidery fears
come crawling out of the corners.
At this late hour,
their webs are shadow-larger
than the facts.

This way, that—
he shifts his weight in bed
the way a traveler does a bag
that's too heavy for him, some load
he can't put down.

His head above his sleep,

he's in the deep end now,
treading water—
all his troubles surfacing,
their ripples widening around him.

In a Mood

She oversleeps
or else she lingers
chin-on-elbow at the breakfast table,
a spoon dragging
in a lumpy porridge of a day.

Next door, a basketball
starts bouncing on the pavement,
that hollow sound,
a boy alone, tossing another hour
through the hoop, pretending otherwise.

It goes on and on,
dangles from her knitting needles,
the wool of winter,
gray and seamless,
one yarn, one stitch like another.

She can't break the pattern,
wants surprise to take her
in a cupped hand and toss her
on the gaming table.
But where should she start—

the blankets on the unmade bed,
the socks on the floor?
She can see the street from her window,
like fruit in a jar
whose lid she can't pry off.

Insomniac

Cares keep cropping up
helter-skelter as the wind-sown
seedlings in his garden.

All night he argues with the wind.
He opens windows,
then he closes them.

He watches bubbles climb
a glass of water.
There is no rushing them.

He sips slowly at the dark
but can't get it down.
Silence keeps him sober.

He listens. Maybe sleep will click,
and close him up,
a jackknife in a firm hand.

The day still spreads before him—
an open map that is hard to fold
on the right lines, hard to put away.

But how easily she sleeps beside him.
She steps out of a day, like a dress,
and drops it on the floor.

Your Recurring Dream

Haven't you noticed
there's often something you can't put away
before you fall asleep
like a necklace that won't unfasten
or pull over your head—something left undone
that nags at you—a white slip of a thought
half-hanging out of a closed drawer?
You dream the way you hold your blue jeans
upside down, shaking them to get
the day's loose change out of the pockets.

If you had nightmares in the last century,
you might have awakened tugging the reins
of some runaway in an open field—
instead of clutching the steering wheel
of your downhill dream—
always speeding, always pushing the brakes
through the floor of consciousness,
night after night, belted
into the same driver's seat,
locked into a dream that never crashes.

The Short

She doesn't give much warning
flaring up
sizzling in her socket
darkening the room for the rest of us.
Stubborn too,
there's no changing her
until she cools down
no shaking the gloom out of her.
A few dark strands keep rattling.

In Praise of Zigzags

For a Girl Failing Geometry

Maybe she does her homework
the way she does her chores.
She moves quickly when she vacuums,
forgetting corners in the living room,
repeating others,
zigzags recklessly across the carpet,
raising those pale tracks
behind her in the wool, crossing
and recrossing them. And not once
does geometry cross her mind.
Outside she wanders aimlessly
behind the lawnmower,
rolls toward the middle of the lawn,
then doubles back.
For a while, she'll follow straight lines—
the fence, the hedge, the walk—
then go off on a tangent, spiraling
around the birch or the maple.
When she finishes,
she leaves the lawnmower out, leaves
a trail of unmown strips and crisscrosses,
her scribbling on the lawn
like a line of thought that's hard to follow.
As far as she's concerned
the shortest distance between two points
is confining.

In Levelled Teaspoons

My daughter's friend
is my friend's daughter, a ten year old,
who while I light the oven
holds her grief as tightly
as I hold the match. She's baking
a cake with someone else's mother—
trying to fill an afternoon
that's bottomless as the sieve
she holds. She sifts
the dry ingredients of loss
into the mixing bowl, then stirs
the flour and sugar until the powder
buries all the crystals.
Huddled over the mix, the two girls
take turns at adding milk
and butter, measuring vanilla,
measuring their words in levelled teaspoons—
while across from them
to make the cake rise, I prepare
the eggs to fold into the heavy batter.
One by one, against the rim,
I crack the shells, separating whites
from yolks, translucency
from opacity, the living from the dead.

In the Runaway's House

She left her bicycle on its side,
the gray fur of the basement growing
on the spokes, the kickstand in the air.

But you keep finding her
the way you come upon a coin or pen
lodged between the cushions of a chair.

Go ahead, hang new curtains in her bedroom,
but you won't break off this thread
between your teeth;

you can paint the walls a different color
and empty the drawers and shelves,
but you can't close the door to this room.

No matter what you do
she keeps taking you by surprise
like the metal hangers jangling in her closet.

Whenever the phone rings, or the doorbell,
you can see her long hair and tinted glasses,
can hear the silk ruffle of her voice.

She's unchanged—the same smile,
the same shirt and faded jeans she left in
fifteen years ago.

Sometimes from the hall, you even see her
at the dressing table, her back to you,
her left hand brushing out her hair,

while like Perseus she is looking at you
in the mirror. She'll never stop,
never get the knots out.

She's fastened in your mind
like a photograph in your album or lines
in a letter that you've read too many times.

At The High School's Winter Musical

Before he sang
some of us in the crowd
didn't know; the program didn't help—
only the song title by his name.
Yet no one laughed as he began.
Even the smaller children
stopped fidgeting in their chairs
to watch him on the stage: a lanky boy,
hands dangling at each side,
eyes on us.

Motionless, we all listened
to his voice surfacing, his soft whine,
like notes urged out of some strange horn,
so frail and eerie,
that love-song mumbled in his own mode.
And when he finished, applause burst out
the way a pile of dry twigs
will flame up all at once; the whole room
ignited—cheering and clapping
that he couldn't hear.

In Your House on Elia Street

If it were summer
when she happened on their empty cottage
in the middle of the woods
and tried their table and their chairs,
their porridge in their bowls,
she might have taken off her shoes afterwards
as I do in your house.
She might have listened for them
when she climbed the stairs that night
or opened drawers—
might have heard what I hear,
turning doorknobs, turning pages
that you've turned.

And if she stayed until the cut flowers
wilted on the mantle,
she might have thrown them out,
holding stems that they had held.
She might have changed the water in the vase
on a murky afternoon, and cut more flowers
for the house, the color of the ones they'd left.
At someone else's sink,
someone else's towel against her face,
she might have hesitated at the mirror
as I do early in the morning,
rubbing off the cold, damp glass,
half-expecting you.

Soft Verge (near Coleshill)

He leans on air
between the hedge and road:
gray hair, gray jacket sagging from his shoulders
and those gray trousers too loose
to prop him up.
All day at the intersection, his wooden hands
dangle from the cuffs, his eyes stare
mask-empty at the traffic.
Motionless,
he slumps for hours,
some slack-jawed puppet hung up clumsily,
loose strings that we can't see
letting his head loll
not just toward his chest
but off slightly to one side.
Nothing moves him. Every day he waits
near the sign-post to the village,
sun or rain on that same stretch of grass,
a stalled car of a man
that nothing can repair. He makes us pause
at the junction, keeps cautioning
like a semaphore stuck in one position.
On our way to town each day,
he's a detour that we don't want to take.

Gaps

She has these spells
that come and go like hiccups,
gaps where moths have feasted
on her wool. Mid-thought, she stops
the way a zipper catches
on a loose thread. She doesn't care.
Behind that habit of a smile,
she's naked now, a fist
with nothing in it. She forgets herself
the way your daughter's knee
forgets its scrape.

Your name, your face—
they're in the glass she spills
without noticing. She's been rolled
in some back alley of her mind,
all her pockets emptied.
She leaves the dining room,
without moving, leaves you
orphaned at the table. No sense from her,
no salt from this soggy-headed shaker:
a few more bites and her table
will be cleared.

The Retreat

Before he turned away
he hoisted the snow shovel,
like a rifle, over his shoulder,
and trudged down the steps, heading back
toward the poor part of town.
From the upstairs window,
I could see him join those other stragglers
out in the street—the small troop,
plowing head-bent into the wind,
like remnants of a retreating army.
Until the street curved,
I could follow his slow progress—
the man at my door, dragging himself
through the snow of another continent,
the floppy boots, the snow-patched
coat and hat of a wounded soldier,
crossing my window, crossing some wilderness
in an old newsreel I can't turn off.

The Trespasser

One slat half-twisted in these blinds
and I can see him out there in the alley
reading through all my trash:
my old shoes, my empty envelopes,
a bare-boned fish.

My thick hedge can't keep him out.
He reads right through it to my dandelions,
my uncut grass. If I'm not careful,
he'll get in the house, brazen past me
like a spider on a house-plant.

In my sitting room
he'll find the white scars
glasses leave on all the tables
and that pale square hanging on the wall.
He won't stop there.

He'll read my favorite chair
like the lines in my palm,
and on my face dark thoughts surfacing
as clothes do in a tub of water.
But I won't talk.

So what if he ransacks every closet
and empties drawers onto the floor.
Shake me, turn me inside-out
like some old sock—
I won't yield.

From a Half-Filled Cup

When he left last night
as quickly as he kissed me on the cheek
some numbness settled over me,
like a cover on a drowsy child,
until this morning
when I cleared the dishes from the dinner table.
His half-filled cup must have
brought the evening back, must have held him,
like some spirit in a magic lamp,
so when I touched the rim, my finger circling
the way a child rubs a crystal glass
to bring the hidden music out,
I thought about his lips, his saliva
in the milky dregs,
and before I carried it to the sink to pour it out—
for a moment, only for a moment—
I thought of drinking
those cold dregs, of drinking more
than what he hadn't,
and of the odd desire
to take that fluid's darkness on my tongue—
a kind of kiss, but colder.

Watermark

In the heat
I have no answer
to your letter.
The ice melts
in my lemonade.
The glass sweats
on the paper.
Your ink
is wet again;
your dark words blur.
They turn the puddle
on the stationery
bruise-blue.
The wet circle
slowly blisters.
It dries
but doesn't heal.

The Regular

Everyone knows her here—
the old trudger with the hem hanging
from her coat. Every day at 2:00,
she traces the same path
through the park, the same dirt-colored
gravel crunching underfoot.

She's been poring over it for years,
one hand pocketed, the other dragging
over the thick privet-hedge,
flicking through it
as you do a book when you can't find
the line you're after.

And who hasn't gone over words
and gestures, scouring an afternoon
like a crucial chapter
to find that page turned down
in youth, the underlinings
of the heart.

Ruth's Surrender

What a strange mood
put its hand on my shoulder
and motioned me to follow her
to this eastern place.
There was no question that day
of turning back toward my mother's house.
Even in the desert, in that midday heat
when we sat on the burning sand
and ate our bread without vinegar,
without shelter from the sun—
drained, foot-weary,
I didn't waver.

I could have turned around before
we reached Bethlehem, before I began
those long days, gleaning wheat
and barley in a stranger's field,
my back bent under the sun's stare,
under the yoke of widowhood.
But I already knew that this was my way.
Washed and anointed, I prepare
myself in solitude. This is my midnight
to meet lying down at the foot of fate
on the threshing floor,
my dark secret from the world.

Horror Vacui

"No nation whose nursemaids were so profligate
with hairpins could survive."
—Emile Zola, on noting hairpins
beneath a bench in Hyde Park

Against some peripety,
some vague, unspoken dread—
she saves old clothes, old letters,
paperbags and paperclips,
rubberbands, corks,
lids without jars, jars
without lids—until every drawer
is stuffed, every closet and shelf
crammed from top to bottom,
the whole house full of collections
like a mind with too much on it.

She cannot discard anything
without vacillating: a torn sheet,
a bent bobby pin, or these black shoes
she hasn't worn for years—
the heels scuffed, the toes
chipped and peeled, like fingernails
that need repolishing; each time
she passes them in the wastebasket,
she can't resist looking in, craning
the way a curious viewer does
over a casket.

The Summons

What led her to my street—
this weathered crone? And why choose
my stoop in the rain? Why my screen door
to sift her words? She won't come in.
Look at her waiting for me:
her crinkled cheeks, her hair
grizzled and uncombed.
She's all purpose on the porch.
She doesn't beg so much
as beckon through the screen,
her sparrow-eyes flitting the whole time.
Our fates know our faces.
They can single us out in a crowd
the way a wolf separates the straggler
from the herd. They follow us home.
This one at the door
travels light—a plastic bag
for a hat, another for a poncho.
She's found my house, found me
as a hermit crab finds an empty mollusk shell.
She's not my size yet—
but she persists. I can see her stratagem:
she doesn't want my empty clothes.
She wants me to cross her threshold.

In Small Rooms

In small rooms
where the aunts are waiting
to join the uncles, they keep
all the windows closed and their valises
ready in the closet like boxes
stacked with empty boxes.

When they stop finger-drumming
on the table, they can hear
the darkness ripening
through the avocado skin, and the uncles
whispering out of photographs,
beckoning to them like faces in water.

But when you visit those tight rooms,
they don't mention it. They wear
confinement like a ring
that won't pull off. One hand warming
on a cup, they drift, stirring the past
slowly through the conversation

as if they're only stirring sugar—
then abruptly, as a piece of cake tumbles
from a fork, they let it drop.
Each morning in a row of saucers
on the window sill, they water
fur-leafed violets faithfully

as you would a cat—
and over their skewbald chairs
they drape the silk shawl
of better times. And who
in such a low-ceilinged room
wouldn't watch the only open door?

Who wouldn't bend a little

toward the mirror, each night
getting closer to the truth, keeping an eye
on it as a guard does a shifty prisoner?
All it takes is a wind, a mere sigh
to lock us out of the house.

The Takeover

At first I thought you were hiding
in another room, waiting
behind a door for just the right moment
to attack—but how slowly
you disclosed yourself:
one vein at a time,
one strand of hair.

I kept thinking I'd recover,
clear my throat of you,
outgrow you like a blackened fingernail,
but you took over. Piecemeal
you got the best of me,
filled my calendar, filled the pages
in my photo album.

It's late. The front door slams again.
I'm no fool upstairs
who thinks you'll settle for the silver
and leave me alone.
I might as well accommodate you.
I set your place at the table.
I lie down with you at night.

The Prognosis

The ink's dried;
the letter's in the mail.

Door to door, the dark rumor
is already metastasizing.

Whoever twists the street signs now
won't throw him off course.

He's the dead reckoner, working
without a compass. He knows her true north,

and she knows what's inside
the package that he brings,

wrapped and ribboned,
the brown spot inside the golden pear.

Windows, doors—
she can't lock this dampness out,

can't shake it off as the dog does rain.
It's in her bones.

Over the dregs, she pours more tea.
She counts the moments of honey

dangling from her spoon.
But she's no match for him.

Night and day, he stares incurably,
follows her from room to room,

follows her outside, a rude guest
who won't say when he's leaving.

With the same breath that blows apart
a dandelion, he keeps whispering her name.

The Last Visit

This room is full of lies:
the bookmark in the book half-read,
the shoes, the suitcase in the closet.
She's not going anywhere.

You can tell by the green
that fills the week-old water
in the flower vase, the bad breath
in the room that no one mentions,

and by the crooked picture on the wall,
the eyes that follow us,
the pools that don't ripple
when a stone drops.

This is the real solitaire,
the whole deck face-up on the table,
no cheating in this game,
no laughing off our losses.

Should we leave now?
They're wheeling carts
and stretchers down the hall,
fresh flowers, fresh faces for the rooms.

She looks at us
but maybe in this walled garden
she can't tell one face from another
like the sparrows we confuse.

Maybe the pain is gone,
and she's as peaceful as the carved pumpkin
on our porch: the fixed look,
the hollow welcome she gives everyone.

If there is a moment of truth

which one is it then—
the mother in the living room
or the one in this white bed?

Tonight after the rain
there's one moon in the sky and one
in the puddle on this empty parking lot.
I don't know which to believe.

The Finishing Touches

While I try on her rings,
her pearls spill
out of a black velvet pouch
into your palm. I can hear them
clicking between your hands
like metal jacks shuffling in our childhood.

Drawer by drawer,
through all her jewelry and her scarves,
her gloves, her handkerchiefs,
the two of us sift slowly,
choosing what we want before packing
the rest in boxes to give away.

Preoccupied,
you still hold that strand,
looping and weaving it around your fingers
before you slip it, cat's cradle-like,
onto mine. The whole exchange
must have taken years,

but how hurriedly
at her closet, grabbing those hangers
by the neck, you sling
that load of clothes over your arm
and cross the room
as if you didn't feel the hollowness

in all those coats and dresses
you were hugging to your chest
or the wire hangers
pressing through the cloth
like neck and shoulder bones in someone frail.
And when you put them near the box,

how matter of fact we are
taking out the hangers, folding
and stacking clothes, the whole time
holding what we cannot grasp.
Wool, cotton, silk—
as if that's all there is to it.

The Necessary Changes

How many times at the dinner table
she pushed words aside
as we might spinach on our plates

or in the middle of an argument
she cleared our places:
a fresh course, a fresh topic.

She took only what she wanted
from our heated talk, skimmed the soup
to leave a lighter broth.

How deftly she avoided facts, like the crumbs
she brushed aside, folding the napkin
from her lap when she'd had enough.

Sometimes in the living room
with no warning, she shifted subjects,
shifting smoothly in her chair,

her stockinged legs crossing
the other way, her hands
hemming a skirt, skirting an issue.

And at his bedside day after day
what else could she do
after she changed the flowers in the vase

but take up knitting needles,
row by row, following that pattern,
pale blue, dark blue.

Mother's Hat

She's sitting at her vanity—three faces
smiling back at her—and I don't know
where I am, but close enough
to smell her perfume
and watch her lift a sheet of tissue paper
out of a flower-printed box,
and then the velvet hat—a small black one
that with a jewel-studded pin
she fastens to her hair.

How vividly it sits,
tilted slightly on her head—
and at the rim, her hands arranging it:
the polished fingernails, the rings.
Then slowly—the way at bedtime
she would pull down the shade
before she left my room—
over her eyes and cheeks, her glossy lips,
she draws down that stiff black veil.

At an Open Half-Door

sfumato . . . used to describe the transitions
of color or, especially, tone from light to dark
by stages so gradual as to be imperceptible.

Months later in the museum
when you stopped in front of Rembrandt's
"Young Girl at an Open Half-Door"
to make the point again,
I remembered
that even while I stood
beside her bed, while I held her hand
in that curtained room, watching
for some sign
and all I could think was MORE—
at the edges of her mouth
and around her eyes, some diffuse light
had already blurred the outlines.
In the painting, as in all
of life's great truths,
wherever the shadow of the room
envelops the girl: on her right side,
along her hair and brow,
her cheek, her lips, her lace-collared neck;
wherever she joins the darkness,
where form rises from its field,
and certainty from uncertainty—
there's no line drawn.

Revenant

Like a dream noise
that wakes you in the night
and makes the house quieter,
it's in the air again—a certain throatiness,
a fluttering, her voice calling
the way ground water pulls
the dowser's hazel wand,
and you want to yell out to her;
you want to open a window
that's painted shut
as if you could catch her on that lawn,
could take her by surprise
like a cat pouncing on a bird.

She won't hold still.
Her laugh flickers through the quiet house—
the off-and-on of music
tantalizing on a car radio,
some distant station you keep losing.
But which is worse,
forgetting or remembering?
Under your breath,
you try rummaging
among the scales for her
as if you could find the right pitch,
the right melody,
as if you could hum her to yourself.

Waiting

Waiting for her
we used to rummage through the drawers
in the living room, making chains
out of paper clips, pleating
old papers into fans. Sometimes
we would dent the dough-soft
cushions on the couch,
would watch them rise.

While someone else cleaned the house,
we would take knickknacks
from the coffee table, arranging them
instead of toys on the carpet,
or leaning cards on cards
we built those flat-roofed houses
that fluttered to the floor, collapsed
our card-thin concentration.

No one taught us. We learned
the physics of that room ourselves,
those aimless specks of light,
our fingerprints on dusty sills. Day by day,
we learned all the properties of waiting—
how it drags a strip of light slowly
over the wallpaper, how like the summer heat
it can't be fanned away.

Out of the Ordinary

First, the milk must boil:
three times the wave of white
rising in the pan,
three times descending;
then before you add
a spoonful of yogurt,
the milk must be no cooler
than your blood,
no hotter. For years,
I've followed the same rules
from some forgotten book,
followed rites that I don't understand—
the wooden spoon,
the thick ceramic bowl—
followed a recipe
as others do religion.
I always stir the warm mix
clockwise in the bowl, always
leave it covered with a plate
on the same window sill
in the kitchen, and by morning
I can always thicken milk
and feed my family
from a bowl of partial knowledge.

The Navel Orange

Before she knew that the navel
is a tiny orange growing in the fruit,
she would peel an orange quickly
as a child tears wrapping from a gift,
a tight knot easier to cut
than an unborn orange,
easier to toss aside.
But this navel orange
that she holds on the cutting board
holds infinities of oranges,
spheres within spheres,
too small to contemplate,
too grand to overlook.

Freeze Warning

I heed cold air
as a floodworker does a river.
I pack up my garden in the dark
to salvage what I can.

Tonight I don't have to choose
between the ripe
and the unready. I can take it all
no questions asked—stem-snapping,

pepper-twisting, these doorknobs
that open nothing, these green
ends-in-themselves.
I like the night-shift, working alone

hours before the killer strikes,
the last chance, the close-call of it.
I like hosta and hydrangea waving their hands,
the ground before it hardens like a corpse.

And walking back, the lights already on
I like having more than I need:
my arms spilling-full of vegetables,
cold and moon-shiny,

tomato leaf smell on my hands.
I like, too, keeping pale tomatoes
on the shelf, turning them red
under my warm eye.

In Flood's Cove

1 Gathering Mussels

At low tide when we walk in this cove
dry rocks clatter
like dishes in careless hands.
But this is no one's sink,
no one's property below the water-line.

Out here, the carpet never dries.
Stringy, full of holes—
it hooks our toes, slips
and squelches like balloons under us
and no one cares. No one waves us off.

The children run ahead
leaving these clues of towels, of buckets
near the water's reach, their shoes
shell-empty on the sand.
They hurdle the icy waves like fences.

Nothing can keep them out.
Shouting, splashing—
they're at home in the mussel beds.
They fill their buckets
and water fills the holes they make.

2 Preparing Mussels

If we're not vegetarians
someone has to kill our dinner—
even the headless bodies
hidden in these shells.

At the kitchen sink
someone has to scrape off barnacles

with a sharp knife
and scrub the shells blue.

Someone has to take each cold mussel
in bare hands
and tear its beard out
like a clothing label.

When the water boils—one of us
must add this tray of sealed envelopes
to steam them open,
to scoop their secrets out.

3 *The Exchange*

We're not finished with dinner
until it's high tide,
not finished with the table
until we put the empty shells
back in the bucket
and take them out though the pines
tacking our way back
to the same rocks where earlier
the tide left mussels out for us.
In the dark, the water comes
half-way to meet us
making it easier
to give the shells back
to toss them from this boulder—
one by one.
A thousand fingers of rockweed
beckon to them. The water
swallows them whole.

The Yield

If we don't pick the brambles clean
along the cliff—what bird-pecking
doesn't torture will hang to death.

Rocks slide in this thicket; branches claw
at our bare arms and legs, but we work fast—
like squatters packing on the sly.

Red-ripe against the green, they make
an easy target—standing still,
at a finger's flick each small head toppling.

Soft and furry raspberries,
right from the bush—unwashed,
unsugared—we down them neat.

No table, no manners here.
There's no host to thank before we leave,
no napkins for our blood-stained hands.

First Seizure

Stiff-legged, the dog kept running,
flapping like a wind-up toy
someone was holding in the air.

He was trying to cross a field
where he couldn't hear us—
uncontrollable as if he'd seen a rabbit.

We couldn't see what was after him,
pinning him down on the bedroom floor
until his legs stopped, then his breathing.

For moments on that dark pool of a rug
he was floating on his side,
fish-like, one eye to the sky,

until how wobblingly—lifting his head,
his body; unfolding his legs
like a foal's—he struggled to his feet

and looked around the room, looked at us.
He couldn't shake that water off.
Bedraggled, spent—he just stood there

like a runaway who reappears
scratching at the back door
after you've given up on him.

Out of the Blue

That May day on the canal we didn't know
which wooden gate would groan
against the water all these years
or which lock hold us in its wet stone walls
so long. That narrow boat
still pulls on the taut rope of memory.
And those herons flapping over us,
wings opening and closing, like umbrellas
in a storm—they can still burst out
of the branches at the strangest times.

Last summer when we walked away
from town along the cliffs, the two of us,
looking down, listening to the sea,
we couldn't tell which white-crested moment
or dark undertow of that long afternoon
might take hold of us.
As carefully as we took each step
out on that ledge, we never knew
which rock, which dizzy spot
might slip into our future.

And on this footpath
where we've stopped to rest in the middle
of the field, waist-high wheat
half-hiding us, dry waves
drowning out our voices,
we don't know which blue moment
will swoop us up in its talons
and which one only circle slowly
before it glides toward
the far corner of the field to disappear
in that green copse.

Revisions on a Postcard

It's that day again—
the wooden table near the road,
the thick socks, the worn trousers
tucked into hiking boots—
and I want to erase my qualms
like a dull entry in a journal.
I want to get up from that terrace table
where we sat in the sun late one afternoon,
writing postcards. This time
over the empty plates and cups,
the beer-stained mugs,
I want to shake the map
wide open on the afternoon
and leave all the unpaid bills behind—
that longing at the edge of town,
like the weight of a backpack
that won't stop pulling.
Before it's too late,
I want to follow the hiker
who got off the bus, slung his pack
over his shoulders, mid-stride,
and without once looking back
left the village on the hill road.

Bedtime, Perdiguier-Haut

When we moved to the house on the hill
with the abandoned winery—
the thick, stone walls,
the room-sized wooden casks—
no one warned us
that if someone knocks on a cask
the spirit of the cave awakens
in the splashing.
Some nights we sit outside
till ten, when an owl
that we've never seen cries out
from the micoucoulier tree near the house—
as if to signal us home.
And who says that daytime
is the waking time?
Lights out, the shutters closed,
I lie in bed, enchanted
like the wine sealed in its cask.
Surely what we can see
must be the lesser part of what we know.
In the dark, I try to imagine
the dreams of the blind,
the wine inside those casks
as blue as blood
before it mixes with the air.
I walk about strange continents at night,
the possibilities spread out
like so many stars.

About the Author

Jane O. Wayne's first book of poems, *Looking Both Ways* (University of Missouri Press), was selected by David Wagoner for the 1988 Devins Award. Her poetry has appeared in publications such as *Poetry, Iowa Review, Ploughshares, The Massachusetts Review, The American Scholar, The Michigan Quarterly Review, Ascent, Poetry Northwest,* and *The Anthology of Missouri Women Writers.* She has taught Creative Writing at Washington University and Webster University in St. Louis, where she lives.